"Marilyn is a maverick networker and r.
Everyone will benefit from Marilyn's knowledge!"

Jo Hausman
International radio show host and best-selling author of *Go For It*

"Marilyn is a strong and caring leader who helps her team become the best they can be! As a part of her team and business partner, I truly enjoy working with her and learn from her every day!"

Dr. Jeffry Life, M.D., PH.D
CEO at The Life Center for Healthy Aging and author of *The Life Plan*

"Marilyn is a maverick in the women's leadership arena!! She is someone who readily seeks to help cultivate leaders in the making and guides them on their journey to success. I've worked closely with Marilyn for several years and witnessed first-hand the empowering skill sets she exudes when leading both individuals and teams to achieve their goals. I couldn't be more proud of such an exceptional human, so if you're looking to lead with authenticity and grace, this book is a must-read!!"

Jessica Crate
Former Olympic Athlete and CEO of Crate Consulting LLC

"Marilyn is an incredible example to women everywhere on how to balance God, love, family, and life's circumstances, while striving to achieve both personal and professional success."

Kevin Messerschmidt
Strategic Health Coach

"It is often said that until someone has walked a path, they cannot properly guide others to do so. That is why we expect this book to help so many people. Marilyn Moser is an overcomer, a leader of leaders, and a follower of God. Her life experiences and wisdom for others are bound to uplift, encourage, and lead so many down their faith path to their God-given destiny. We highly recommend this book!"

Mark and Lori Welch
Entrepreneurs and Lead Pastoral Team of The Pointe Church in Antelope, CA

"Once upon a time, Marilyn Moser's life was turned upside down by this mysterious, exquisite thing called grace—and there was no turning back. Her unwavering belief in the promises of God is absolutely contagious whenever she speaks, leads, or writes. Today, her unquenchable passion to make a difference in the lives of others has transformed her into a powerhouse for Jesus. I can't wait to see what happens next."

Jennifer Dukes Lee
Grace Dweller, Storyteller, and Author of *Love Idol* and *The Happiness Dare*

"Marilyn Moser is an amazing woman in the women's leadership arena. I have worked closely with Marilyn for over 20 years in the healthcare field where her energy and enthusiasm for helping others shows through on a daily basis. She is a God-fearing woman who devotes her life to her family, friends, co-workers, and patients. She is a talented leader with a positive attitude and is a joy to all who she surrounds."

Sharon Wartenbee, RTR, BD, CBDT, ASRT

"Marilyn is an incredible woman full of life! Her energy and enthusiasm for helping others is amazing. Marilyn's positive attitude and optimism is contagiously uplifting! God has given her many talents that she continues to develop and freely shares."

Beth Weber, MPH, RT (R), RDMS, CRA, FASRT
Director of Imaging Services and HIPAA Privacy Officer at Avera Heart Hospital

"Marilyn is a model of servant leadership. She embodies all the aspects of fostering success in herself and in those around her. She has overcome many obstacles to achieve her own success in her personal and business lives. Learn from her to help you achieve your own dreams."

Dr. Mark Gordon, MD, FACC
Functional Medicine Cardiologist and Business Partner

"You'll never meet another person with Marilyn's spunky spirit and her fervor for life. She has a heart for women and yearns to impact the lives of those around her by sharing her powerful story. As busy women, we often miss the shift of priorities in our lives and it leaves us feeling like we're not enough ... like we've somehow failed our husband, children, and ourselves. Marilyn recognized the shift in her own life, sought out the truth, and now walks in the grace that every woman craves ... the grace she gives herself. Through Marilyn's story, I've gained confidence, courage, and am empowered to walk in my own grace."

Lisa Brouwer
CEO of Full Throttle Living, Keynote Speaker and Coach

"Marilyn Moser pours her poise and passion into helping others build purpose in their lives. Her energy and fun personality will draw you in while reading this book, allowing you to find the key to what really matters in life. Buckle up for a great ride!"

Jim Schaeffer
Author of *Wolves, Sheep and Sheepdogs* and CEO of JCS and Associates, Inc.

"Marilyn has poured her heart into this book to help you achieve those dreams that you have stashed away. Through her life's experiences and facing her fears, she takes you on a journey of empowerment. Enjoy the ride to GRACE."

Maria Williams
Entrepreneur and Motivational Speaker

MARILYN MOSER

Code to Grace

UNLOCKING

GOD'S REDEEMING LOVE

IN YOUR LIFE

THRONE
PUBLISHING GROUP

Throne Publishing Group
2329 N Career Ave #215
Sioux Falls, SD 57107
ThronePG.com

DEDICATION

My legacy—
    I dedicate this book to my dear family, my beloved husband, and children. You are precious gifts to me and I love you forever and always ....

—Marilyn

CONTENTS

INTRODUCTION

Isn't it funny how we remember some distinct, seemingly "every-day moments" from our childhood that somehow turn out to shape our future? My third grade teacher in 3-C at good ole West Lyon Community School used to read us a story after lunch every day. She would rock up and down on her tiptoes in front of the class as she shared the story. One day, she asked everyone to take out a piece of paper and draw what we wanted to be when we grew up.

I drew a big book and wrote in BOLD crayon, "AUTHOR!"

Who would've thought that years later that is just what I'd do?! The idea of telling my story began as a series of "God winks" that put certain people in my path who guided me through this—what I feel has been a God-directed endeavor. I feel led to write this book, not because I am "qualified" or an expert or because I've got it "all figured out." Trust me, I don't! I do not claim to have a perfect life, but I instead I want to use my mistakes and mess ups to help others make better choices or to avoid what I have experienced. I feel called to use my pain for a purpose, and I want to encourage you to forge ahead, follow your heart, and live with assurance and grace. I know you are capable of creating the life you were designed to live. It's your turn, and it's not too late. Today is just the right time to start! Follow me … I'll show you the way!

My brokenness is a better bridge for people than my pretend wholeness ever was.

—Sheila Walsh

PART ONE

MY MEADOWS

1

MEADOWS

My story began in the quaint little town of Lester, Iowa, a small, friendly, and pleasant farming community. There are no stoplights or traffic jams here, and there is surely more pasture than concrete. Like many small Midwestern towns, on Main Street there is a bank, a post office, and a fire department where my dad was the fire chief. There is a grocery store, a grain elevator, where my mom worked part-time as a bookkeeper, and Louie's Cafe on the corner with a seasoned grill so you get the best burgers made just right.

I had a modest, middle-class upbringing. My parents worked hard, and we lived in a big, two-story house on a corner lot in town with a big front yard. My dad loved planting a large garden, and my three sisters and I would take turns weeding and picking produce each summer. We did a lot of canning and learned the value of teamwork and appreciating the simple things in life.

My dad worked at the meat packing plant while my mom stayed home to raise us. She also did some babysitting from home and typed thank-you letters for a car dealership. We were a happy, loving, busy family. We would have picnics or family potlucks and attend socials with our church community, playing Red Rover and Kick the Can. I loved the parades every summer, games at the ball diamond, swimming lessons, summer rec, and our town's big, annual celebration—Lester Days.

Every year, we would take a family vacation to visit our cousins in Illinois. My sisters and I looked forward to this trip like we looked forward to Christmas! We'd pack the back end of our Kingswood Estate woodgrain-sided station wagon with blankets, pillows, games, and snacks for the 8-hour trip across Iowa. The next morning, we would get up early to leave. I'll always remember chanting aloud "M-I-S-S-I-S-S-I-P-P-I!" as we crossed the Mississippi River toward the Illinois state line. It was a special time in my childhood.

We'd spend a whole week with our relatives riding our bikes to the swimming pool, staying up late to watch movies, and going to Six Flags theme park for thrills. My Aunt Mary loved to organize scavenger hunts for us around the city of Peoria, which were always so much fun. I cherish the wonderful memories we made as carefree cousins.

As a family, we had everything we needed.

As a family, we had everything we needed. Our parents always taught us that faith and family trumps everything, and it did. I was a small-town, Christian girl who always felt loved, safe, connected, and grounded. There was a sense of trust, authenticity, and warmth there, and it gave me peace.

ENTREPRENEURIAL GIRL

I did well in school and looked forward to seeing my friends each day, but I enjoyed free time after school even more when my active imagination could run free. As soon as my chores were done, I played around town with my friends. We would put pennies on the railroad tracks or play down by the mud creek, and we loved exploring old, abandoned buildings. We'd always keep busy, and it was okay with our parents that we were having "play dates" as long as we were home by the 6 o'clock whistle for supper. In those hours, the town was magical, and it was ours.

We would set up lemonade stands on Main Street and organize parades around town, decorating our bikes just to ride up and down the streets. It was fun setting up carnivals in our big front yard, too, or picking rocks out of people's driveways, then painting them and selling them back. I was not one to sit and play with dolls; I felt happiest when I was creating something.

As I look back, I recognize an entrepreneurial spirit that is still very alive within me today. I see an entrepreneur as someone who creates and builds systems or businesses; someone who builds from their own dream.

An entrepreneur finds a need and then fills it.

An entrepreneur finds a need and then fills it. They look around and ask, *"What is missing here? What do people need or want?"* This is what I was doing with my friends on the streets of Lester, and it was a wonderful time.

I have a special admiration for female entrepreneurs because we have that motherly, nurturing instinct to help people. We are very relational and know how to build a community. I think entrepreneurs also believe in someone before that person may even believe in themselves. They take time to find gifts or talents in people that they may not see in themselves, and then draw that out of them.

To this day, I love doing that for others. It's rewarding to find unique ways to encourage them and see them succeed. But along with my creative spirit, I struggled with insecurity and fear.

ENCOUNTERING FEAR AND ENCOUNTERING GOD

In my middle school years especially, I had anxiety. To this day, I don't know why that was, but I experienced palpable fear. There were days that the fear and anxiety affected me so much that I didn't want to go to school or sometimes I wanted to leave school early. Some days I was so afraid, I couldn't even sit in the lunchroom with the kids. It was very real, but so was my faith. During those anxious times, I would always pray. No matter how large or small the fear was, I remember having the sense that God was with me.

That was a given, and it was enough.

Throughout the years in school, I had lots of friends and stayed involved in activities. I was involved in band, music, and speech and was a cheerleader in high school. I loved being social and encouraging others. As an adult, I have experienced that same fear I had as a young girl, but for the most part, I outgrew the anxiety.

Overall, I was happy and adventurous, but I also knew I was quite different from my sisters. Our family attended church and Sunday school every week like most everyone else in Lester. Sunday was for church, and we would always attend the morning and afternoon service. We were a strong, Christian family.

Although I knew I was confident in my relationship with Jesus, there was one day in my childhood that continues to stand out to me. I used to play in this meadow—a big horse pasture behind our neighbor's house across the street; coincidentally, this is the same pasture behind the community church we attend today. One day, I went out there alone, as I usually did, just to play in the open space. Suddenly, I had this thought of, *Where did time begin? Where was God in the beginning?* I was just a young girl, but I had this powerful sense of familiarity, as if I had been in that space with God before, and I felt God's peace surrounding me.

God was so real to me in that moment. I was young, but everything around me felt good, secure, and safe. I felt free. And anytime I ever felt that paralyzing fear from anxiety creep into my heart again, I would think on the meadow, envisioning the open sky and the peace that had come over me, and I would feel as though I

> **I felt God's peace surrounding me.**

was surrounded by the presence of a Loving Father.

From the meadow to the lemonade stands and ball games, the small, friendly, farming community of Lester was filled with wonderful experiences. My childhood was good to me, and I was a happy girl. It's where I came to know myself and where I came to rely on

God, but there was no way I could have known that my relationship with Him was only beginning.

Soon enough, I would be seeking His Provision in a much deeper way …

CHAPTER 1: REFLECTIONS

1. Reflect on your childhood. How has it shaped you today?

2. How were you entrepreneurial as a child?

3. **Do you see parts of your childhood or hometown that have shaped your career?**

PART TWO

MY RELATIONSHIPS

2

REAL-ATIONSHIPS

G rowing up, I knew what it meant to be part of a church community, and I'm grateful to my parents for teaching me that. To me, it is a family of God's people who serve as a nurturing support system on your Christian walk. This community guides you and keeps you accountable, and there is a healthy structure in place.

Although I had a strong relationship with my church family, it wasn't until later in my life that I began to understand what it meant to have a relationship with God. I gained a deeper understanding of the difference between a *religion and a personal relationship*. It took me a long time to trust that my connection with God was my own to covet, and a "specific" church membership was not required for my relationship to be authentic.

There are two poignant moments in my life that have become a real testimony to this realization, and it is these two stories that together began a journey of discovering God's true gift of outrageous grace.

FEAR COMES AGAIN

It was 1985, and the weather was surprisingly mild for January. The moon was high and bright in the sky. My husband, Joel, and I were dating at the time, and we were riding in a car with three of our friends. We were just out cruising the gravel roads and listening to the 80's cassette tape "Honeymoon Suite." The night was coming to a close, so we dropped off two of our friends. It was just Joel and me in the back with our friend driving us home. Suddenly my friend lost control of the car. She veered off the road into an approach, and the car flipped end-over-end in a rollover. We landed on the wheels, but the whole top was completely crushed. It seemed as though each flip of the car was in slow motion. I could hear the sound of the glass breaking and the car crunching each time we hit the cold, hard ground. Then there was only a dead silence. Thankfully, Joel and the driver were both responsive, but they were trapped inside the mangled car. My adrenaline had kicked in, and I was thinking to myself, *Where are we?* I was not that familiar with the country road, but, even though I was dazed, I was able to get free through a broken window. I crawled out and ran for help.

The nearest farmhouse was only a quarter mile away, and I could see a glimmer of the yard light in the distance. As I was running toward rescue, I was praying out loud, "Please, God, help us!" Even in that moment when I was scared, in shock, and worried for my boyfriend and my friend, I felt protected. There was so much chaos and fear, but I felt as if I was being carried to the farmhouse.

When I got to the house, we called an ambulance. When they arrived, the emergency crew had to use the Jaws of Life to get Joel and the driver safely extracted from the twisted car wreck. We all were taken to the hospital and after a couple days, everyone was released. Thankfully, there were no serious injuries, but it's still amazing to me how blessed we all were to be alive. Even the insurance adjuster later said, by the looks of the car, we should not have survived an accident of that magnitude. I truly feel angels were watching over us.

> **I truly feel angels were watching over us.**

After the night of the accident, fear returned into my life, and it only escalated from there. I started feeling the anxiety that I'd had as a girl creeping back into my heart. Life was taking me on a different course than I had ever expected.

THE CHALLENGER

It was the fall after the accident. Joel and I got married, and we moved to Sioux Falls where I was attending radiologic technology school full time. It was supposed to be an exciting time in my life. But we were young—I was only 19 years old!—life was moving so fast, and our marriage was new. Like many couples, we were finding the new "us" and working to understand who we were becoming as a couple and how to navigate the expectations of our parents and others.

Then January 28, 1986, happened. Most of us remember where we were when we heard Elvis had died or what we were doing when the towers fell on 9/11, but I remember distinctly where I was on the day of the Challenger explosion.

I was alone in our little basement apartment when the RCA tube TV started screeching of a "Special Report." At 10:39 a.m., the space shuttle Challenger broke apart 73 seconds into its flight, killing all seven crew members. As the news stations reporting from the Kennedy Space Center kept replaying footage of the explosion into the blue Florida sky, I just stood there, in a fog, watching.

I was horrified and devastated as they listed the names of the astronauts on board. Moreover, it felt as if my own life was caving in at that moment, and I couldn't take any more hurt. I realize now that the difficult circumstances in my life didn't matter—what mattered was that I was losing who I was and the simple, authentic relationship with God I so desperately desired.

I was hurting because, even though I was raised to believe in a mighty God, I didn't understand why asking Jesus into my heart and having conviction in my salvation with Him had to be so complicated. I just wanted to trust and believe that simple promise of God's saving grace. But instead I felt abandoned, scared, and alone, and I knew that any decisions or actions I made at that point would have been out of fear.

Thankfully, I remembered the verse from Romans I had heard as a child: "Anyone who calls on the name of the Lord shall be saved." When we were young, I used to listen a Christian radio show every Saturday morning, and I recall so fondly putting that verse on my heart for a time such as this.

And it was enough.

Suddenly that verse was all I needed to finally realize it was about God and me. None of the other stuff mattered anymore! Up until that moment, I was trying so hard to please everybody and prove myself worthy; finally, I was able to eliminate all expectations and fear. I understood fully that His love for me is unconditional and my relationship with Him isn't about performance or earning His acceptance. It is just about God and me and not a Religion, and that's all I needed!

Recalling the verse from Romans reminded me to trust in God's promises and take confidence in them. From there, I was able to overcome the fear and anxiety that had been crippling me. It wasn't long before my marriage was strong again and I was equipped with a new spiritual assurance. I started learning about God's grace through a community of people and mentors who taught me the fullness of God's unconditional love. That knowledge empowered me and quieted my fear and feelings of inadequacy. I began to understand that I was enough. I wasn't perfect, but, through God's grace and love, I was enough.

And this is what I hope for you, too. I want you to know that you are loved. You have gifts that will undoubtedly serve a greater purpose and help you live out your calling. And you, too, are worthy

You have gifts that will undoubtedly serve a greater purpose and help you live out your calling.

of God's outrageous and abundant love and forgiveness. His unbelievable gift of saving grace is simply waiting for you! We begin that relationship by asking Him into our heart and surrendering our life to His Sovereign plan. When we "Let Go and Let God," our life seems to find a rhythm of peace and we can rest in the assurance that He wants us to live in His full abundance and grace.

One of the first steps that will help you in this journey is to find a community of believers who accept you for who you are and who you aspire to be. Surround yourself with people who give you grace as you grow. Accept their support and guidance. Love them, too, but your relationship with God should come first because, in the end, it's about you and Him. Philippians 1:6 says, "He who began a good work in you will carry it on to completion until the day of Christ Jesus." Find your own peace with God in a place that is nurturing, kind and healthy, and trustworthy. You will grow and thrive in His grace; you will be encouraged by your community of believers, and you will thrive.

Just like my day in the meadow, just like my walk toward rescue after the accident, and just like that day alone in the basement apartment, God reassured me of His presence, and I felt His boundless love and grace. I hope this for you, too.

CHAPTER 2: REFLECTIONS

1. Who is your faith community? How have they guided you?

2. Reflect on times of fear in your life. What was your overcoming moment?

3. Do you have any scripture or mantras that have guided you in your life? List them here, and give thanks for their counseling.

3

MOTHER-SHIP

My husband and I were young when I was first pregnant. Admittedly, I was a little scared. I was just finishing radiologic technology school and would soon be completing my ARRT Board exam and need to look for a job. Was I even "qualified" to be a good mom? Like many first-time moms, I remember doubting myself and feeling insecure, wondering if I could even handle the great responsibility of caring for a precious human being.

But God must have felt I was qualified because the moment I learned I was expecting my son, the love I felt was the most incredible feeling in the world! I was in awe of how I could love this baby so much when I hadn't even held him yet. This is when I started to understand the power of God's love in a new way.

When you carry a child, you feel an unconditional love toward that child, and they didn't do anything to deserve it. You don't love them under certain conditions, you simply love them from the moment they are conceived. My first born son was just in my womb, existing and abiding, but I loved him unconditionally, and I realized then that God loves us in the same way. Romans 5 says, "God shows His love for us in that while we were still sinners, Christ died for us." Despite our faults or our failures, God loves us, in much the same way as mothers love their babies.

You don't love them under certain conditions, you simply love them from the moment they are conceived.

That feeling was reinforced when our son was born. Holding my newborn son changed my heart forever. The incredible joy of being a mother was such a privilege. Even though I didn't know how to be the perfect mom, I knew that, with love and faith, I would figure it out and God would guide me along the way. We fell in love again six years later when we had our beautiful baby girl. I remember my mother-in-law holding her and saying, "Now you have the million-dollar family—a boy and a girl!" And we felt like she was right. We loved our sweet family, and being young parents was an incredible, priceless journey, and hands down much better than a million dollars!

THE HAND THAT ROCKS THE CRADLE
RULES THE WORLD

Motherhood is a huge honor for me, and I'm grateful to my own mothers who not only mentored me along the way, but set an incredible example to pursue as I raised my own children.

My mom was entrepreneurial in her own way while we were growing up. I loved seeing her be creative in helping to contribute to the family finances. She was always willing to bring in her own income through different part-time jobs. Along with her bookkeeping work and thank-you letters, she also was involved in a home-based business and sometimes she would have ladies over for "color sessions," where they would buy household products and personal care items such as makeup from her. Even though she didn't like to wear makeup, she was always helping people look and feel their best. I also like helping people feel and look their best! I guess in regard to wearing makeup, as the saying goes, if the barn needs painting, then paint it!

Creativity in finances was just one of the things I admired about my mom. She exemplified strength to me, too, when she was diagnosed with breast cancer. Thankfully, because she was faithful about getting her screening mammograms, she caught it early. She was advised to have a lumpectomy, then radiation treatments. I would go to doctor appointments with her, and I remember admiring her strength as she endured the treatments. She quieted her fears with her great faith and courage, despite losing her own mother to breast cancer. I am so proud of how brave she was in the face of that terrifying diagnosis. And I'm so thankful to be able to say that she is a survivor.

Not everyone can say that they admire their mother-in-law but I can go even a step further. My mother-in-law also was a role model to me. She had an incredible zest for life! We were very close. She never treated me as in-law, but as her own daughter. She was positive, warm and friendly, a beloved nurse at the local hospital, and a great example of grace and unconditional love for my children and me. No matter what her children put her through, she never rejected them and instead loved them through anything. That was a powerful lesson to me.

Because Joel's parents only lived a mile down the road from us, our children had a lot of "grandma and grandpa" time growing up, and I'm so grateful for that today. We all went to church together, they were always there to help us, and we felt their love and support along our parenting journey. We lost both of Joel's parents early in their lives, and I realize now that God gave them such a big role in our family because they wouldn't be with us long.

WHAT MOTHERHOOD TAUGHT ME

I learned so much from my mothers, but it's uncanny to me to realize how much motherhood would teach me and guide me in my professional life today.

> So much of running a business is about pulling out people's strengths and gifts.

The way we nurture our children as we raise them is great practice for how we should nurture a team or a business. As mothers, we are a community of women encouraging and guiding our family. As professional adults, we are businesswomen building community as well.

Most importantly, so much of running a business is about pulling out people's strengths and gifts and believing in them before they may even believe in themselves. It comes naturally for us because we do the same thing for our toddlers and young children. When they are learning to walk or ride a bike, play the piano or learn a new sport, we are constantly instilling our belief in their abilities to succeed. And then when they are successful, they are so surprised and excited! As moms, we are right there to say, "See? You did it! Good job! I knew you could do it!"

As mothers, we are our children's first cheerleader. We see the best in our children and support them. Those same things are what I practice in my business and for my team today. I love seeing a skill or gift in someone that they may not have realized yet. I enjoy encouraging them as they hone that skill and become proficient in it. And when they succeed, I love being able to celebrate with them!

Another lesson we can glean from motherhood is to take care of ourselves. Motherhood can be exhausting, which is why it is so important to not lose sight of who you are. I remember reading parenting books or attending Bible studies, but I don't think I poured into myself with personal development as much as I should have. I don't think I made time to pour into myself physically, emotionally, and spiritually. And the time goes by so fast! Years passed quickly, and I realized I was shorting myself of what I needed.

When you are raising a family, you can so easily lose focus on what your passions are or what your purpose may be, and soon enough the kids leave for college and there is a huge void in your life. You can easily find yourself wondering, *What is my significance in this world? Who am I? Who is my husband and what will our relationship look like now?* This is why it's so important to practice personal development, take quiet time for yourself to intentionally discover what makes you tick, and be patient with yourself, too. These habits take time to develop. Daily making time for what you need and who you want to become takes practice. I found that I had to give myself a little grace, just as I afforded others. Each new day was an opportunity to become more of who I wanted to be, taking the time to do the things that helped me to become that person. As I learned and practiced these steps, I felt like God gave me a "wink" as I figured out how to find success at home and work.

When you are trying to meet your family's needs on a daily basis, it's hard not to feel overwhelmed. But you can quiet that feeling when you take one thing at a time. Just as you go through your daily chores of doing laundry, making dinner, and getting your children to their practices, you can create business activities that lead you to success. I learned that both daily goals and long-term goals can help you feel accomplished along the way. And just like in the business world, if you can do just one little thing each day—check something off your list—it's a huge step in moving forward. Then, over time, those little disciplines build success. This is how parenting works, and it works professionally, too. Carve out 15 minutes each day for personal development and you will find this is well worth the time.

GROWING ROOTS AND WINGS

As I look back on raising my kids, I realize I wasn't always a patient mom or the perfect mom, but I have loved my children unconditionally. I have always been their soft place to land. I tried to let them know: *You are welcome here, in my arms, and you are always accepted here. This is where you can grow your roots and your wings.* I did my best to instill a sense of grace and belief in them, knowing I was here for them, where they are rooted. And that I would always encourage them to fly, to succeed.

We have an enormous, century-old cottonwood tree on our farm that I find symbolic. It stands over 60 feet tall and has a circumference of 17 feet—I had Joel measure it! One summer, Joel was trimming old trees around our acreage, and he was going to hire someone to cut down that big cottonwood tree. Luckily, I found out about it before that gigantic tree saw the ax! That tree has endured many storms in its lifetime—all sorts of tests and trials similar to what we, too, sometimes face. But just the cottonwood, I want our children and our grandchildren to know that they have deep "roots" here at home and also "wings" to go anywhere they choose to soar in life. When they see that tree on our farm, I hope they are reminded of the strength and endurance our family roots bear. And just as that tree reaches into the sky, I want them to reach for their dreams, knowing their family believes in them. And if they don't succeed, I want them to know that grace and unconditional love are practiced here. I want them to feel like home is a place of security, safety, protection, and forgiveness.

> I want our children and our grandchildren to know that they have deep "roots" here at home and also "wings" to go anywhere they choose to soar in life.

Like most families, we've had our share of trials and tests over the years. But just as the massive cottonwood stands firm on our farm, I am reminded of David Timms' book, "Living the Lord's Prayer." In it, he talks about "putting down roots and learning to give and take of community." He shares that grace can only flourish when it encounters offense, that forgiveness requires conflict, healing emerges from hurt, and strength arises from struggle. This reminds me not only of motherhood, but of our family roots. We will go through hardship together, but through forgiveness and reconciliation, we choose the same unconditional love that God has for us.

Together, we choose grace.

"All things work together for good to those who love God, to those who are called according to His purpose." (Romans 8:28)

CHAPTER 3: REFLECTIONS

1. If you are a parent, take time here to reflect on raising your children. What are your fond memories?

2. Who has counseled you in parenthood?

3. How do you grow yourself? If you're seeking self-care, list here steps you can begin today.

4

GREEN ACRES

Joel and I met in first grade, in Mrs. Tomjack's class. He was the shy farm boy, and I was the outgoing town girl. I remember he gave me a pretty blue ring on the playground at recess, but he was always so quiet around me! As we got older, he would literally stare at me in class, so I finally told his best friend Lance, "Either tell Joel to stop staring at me or just ask me out!" So he asked me out, and we double dated after a basketball game to Pizza Hut with our friends Rob and Michelle.

We didn't start dating until our senior year; immediately, he was this person I had known forever. Our relationship felt comforting from the get-go, and it continues to feel that way today. We were the epitome of opposites attract and like to joke about how "we are the Green Acres couple," "he was a little bit country and I was more rock 'n roll," "he was about the chores and I was about the stores," or "we're the tangle of barbed wire and lace." In a crazy way, we were meant to be.

But it's not easy to love a farmer. In fact, it's damn hard! And the farming/ranching lifestyle was hard on our marriage, too. But the attributes that make him a great person and farmer are also what I love and admire most about my husband. His heart is so soft despite his rough persona. Even though we've been through a lot of ups and downs and struggles together over the years, his love for me is unconditional, and I'm so grateful for him.

I'm so grateful for my farmer.

DIRTY FINGERNAILS

Joel always has dirt under his fingernails. His dad did, too. But they tell a story that soft, clean hands can't. They are the hands that work the soil and grease the engines, pull calves and fix the barbed wire fence. These are not manicured hands; in the calluses, I see compassion. I see a farmer's hands; one who tends the soil, a steward of the land, a caregiver to his animals. My Joel.

In the calluses, I see compassion.

There's something centering about living in the open country, on a farm, when you're connected to the earth, wind, rain, and sun as a means of living. Just like our cottonwood, it's grounded to the roots of the earth. You grow up knowing your food doesn't come from the grocery store; it comes from the soil. And the soil is worked by the hands of the "steward of the land."

There is power in knowing that you rely on a mighty benevolent God, the Creator of the universe, for growing of the crops that feed the world. It's the faith and humility of completely surrendering the outcome to that Creator, preparing the soil, planting the seed, and expectantly waiting for the rain and the sun to produce the crop. Then, as harvest season approaches, you thank God for keeping up His end of the deal. "I'll plant, you help it grow," says the farmer, and then you repeat the process over and over as seasons change. Just as the verse in Ephesians reminds us, "To everything, there is a season."

> **There's no doubt about it, farming takes faith.**

When you're engaged in the profession of farming, you have to rely on the Creator's hand, and that's humbling and terrifying at the same time. There's no doubt about it, farming takes faith. Joel has that faith, and it's one of the things I admire about him. Let me tell you about another one.

Do you remember the Waylon Jennings song, "Mammas, Don't Let Your Babies Grow Up to be Cowboys"? He must've known that the boys who raise cows are cut from a different mold. Because even though I don't believe in reincarnation, I swear my hubby was a "bovine" in another life! He is so connected to his herd of cows that it's a little "spooky." He can often sense when they are having trouble calving or he's got a newborn calf drowning in the creek or their head is stuck in the gate. Let me share a few examples of his "sixth sense" when it comes to his cattle.

One afternoon, Joel sent me a text me while I was at work that said, "Thank God for broken windows!" I wondered what he meant by that, and he explained that he had shattered the tractor window while mowing at the other farm and was upset he had to go back to get the mess of broken glass cleaned up. But when he drove back to our yard, he noticed a young calf almost lifeless with his head stuck in the gate and gasping for breath. Joel was able to get the calf free, but it was a close call. That broken glass helped to save the calf!

Another time, Joel was gone from the yard but had a hunch he needed to go back home to check on the calves in the pasture. Sure enough, one of the new calves was almost drowning in the thick mud by the creek that runs through the pasture. He has this "sixth sense" when he's in calving mode, and it's incredible.

True cowboys like my husband don't always dress the part—they don't always wear cowboy hats and belt buckles, or even Tony Lama boots or Stetson hat attire—you can just tell them by their heart. Rugged and untamed. It's who he is, his very being, and I came to learn just what it meant for him to be able to be true to himself and his passion.

When we were younger, I never understood why farming and raising cattle were so important to Joel, but then, when we lived in Sioux Falls in that tiny basement apartment, it began to make sense. Living in the city, there were times when it seemed that Joel needed this oxygen he wasn't getting. It was so hard for him to adjust to the city, the traffic, the noise and the neighbors, and it was just too much cement! It was almost as if he felt he couldn't breathe there. When we finally moved to our farm in the country, he was home. He was back to the land where his grandfather and dad had farmed, where his deep roots were planted for his own purpose in life. When I saw that transformation in his demeanor, it clicked for me. I understood that this is where he needed to be. This is where he was meant to be and felt like he was his best self.

I call it his "Zone of Genius." Joel and I recently watched the old movie "City Slickers," and in that movie there is a scene where Curly and Mitch deliver a calf together. It was a turning point in the movie where their purpose in life became perfectly clear, and that reminds me of my husband. When you are in your "Zone of Genius," you are fully alive, and I envied Joel for that. He had found what I was still seeking.

Watching him shine on the farm and amid his cattle used to make me wonder, *What's my purpose? What's my Zone of Genius?* I knew my career as a radiologic technologist helped to pay the bills, but it wasn't my true calling. I loved my calling as a wife, mother, sister, daughter, and friend, but where did my "Zone of Genius" lie?

When our kids were small, I worked part-time at the local hospital and took aerobic classes from a great instructor named Lois. I remembered how it felt to take the classes and debated the thought of teaching them. And that got me thinking that it would be fun to enroll in fitness instructor training and learn to lead classes, too, so I did! I led classes for surrounding communities and encouraged ladies to get in shape and feel better about themselves, and I loved it. Just like the cheerleader I was in high school, it was an opportunity for me to encourage others and "cheer them on," and it felt as if I was in my Zone of Genius. I found a place where my passion met a career opportunity, and it felt great! Joel and I were content in our respective places, but that didn't mean that things were always easy.

Just like everyone else, we had to work to make our life together a success as well. Farming and ranching were especially challenging in those early years, and Joel and I both worked full-time jobs outside of the farm operation to make ends meet. Eventually, it took its toll on our marriage and parenting, so we were fortunate to have guidance from good Christian friends and neighbors to help us when times were tough.

AN INTENTIONAL MARRIAGE

Marriage isn't easy, but if there is anything loving a rugged farmer has taught me, it's to keep going, to never give up on your spouse, and to respect one another for all they are and all they aspire to be. Support one another through whatever it is they love, and empower each other along the way. These truths ring true for us throughout the year but during harvest more so than the rest of the year. It's a season that's long on hours and short on time together.

During harvest, I always worry about my hubby being out there "alone," but one morning he sent me a text message that continues to encourage me today. His text said:

"Thank you, Lord, for this beautiful day to harvest. Thank you for your blessing on this farm, Your farm. Thank you for this old combine that seems to almost sing when I'm pushing this bountiful crop through her. All things that I know I'm helpless

without your guiding Hand. Continue this journey with me,
Lord. ... See? I'm not harvesting alone.
     Love, Joel"

I like to think God gave me a "wink" that day when I read that message. He knew Joel was right for me.

My husband inspires me. Even though I'm not the perfect farm wife, he has learned just how to accept and love me over the years. Careers and other challenges can be hard on a marriage, but we have learned we are better when we stick it out together. We know that it may not be easy, but it will be worth it! When life gets tough, try to see the bigger picture, trust the bigger vision, and hang in there, together. When you stick it out, you will see the reward on the other side. Just like in running a business, be patient with the time, the work, and the effort it takes, and know there are big rewards on the other side. Remember, everything worthwhile in life takes time, endurance, and patience. Marriage is no exception.

When you are together, in love and in faith, there are always blessings of bounty awaiting.

CHAPTER 4: REFLECTIONS

1. Give thanks for your spouse or business partner. What characteristics in them have you come to appreciate?

2. How do you respect your partner's career? How can you be better?

3. In marriage, or in any relationship in your life, how do you offer support?

PART THREE

MY EMPOWERMENT

5

SHERPAS

I think one of the most powerful ways to change someone's life is to be a mentor. I've always valued the role that mentors have played in my own life and find that they have been significant in my personal and professional growth. Today, I can't stress enough how important it is to have mentors in your life and to act as a mentor for someone else.

When I was at a conference once, I was introduced to the term "Sherpa." In definition, a Sherpa is a member of a Himalayan people renowned for their skill in mountaineering. During this presentation, they referred to acting as a Sherpa once you have achieved a certain level of leadership in business. Just as a Sherpa is a knowledgeable, helpful guide in the

> **I can't stress enough how important it is to have mentors in your life and to act as a mentor for someone else.**

mountains, we, too, have an opportunity to guide and lead a team as their "Sherpa."

I loved the analogy. A Sherpa is just like a mentor, someone who pulls you up and guides you through paths in life. Sherpas help you find your way and make it through successfully. They are responsible and wise. If you want to be successful—whether during your mountain climb or in life in general—you must have a Sherpa by your side. It reinforced my belief in the power of mentors and the impact they have. It reminded me of how much the mentors in my life impacted me in my business and who I had become.

As you look at your life, you may see mentors in people that you didn't credit that title to before reading this. You may already have people in your life who have impacted you in a positive way and for whom you are thankful.

If not, it's okay to seek out a mentor now. I would say that it's imperative to find one who you can trust and who will guide you as a Sherpa would. Your mentor will have a number of admirable qualities, just as the Sherpa does. They can be trusted to lead you toward your goals, have good relational skills, are healthy for you to be around,

They do not force; rather they teach and guide you in kindness and love.

and empower you by creating a space for you to grow, excel, and be your best. They do not force; rather they teach and guide you in kindness and love.

MY PERSONAL SHERPA

My mother-in-law was a great mentor and role model in my life. We worked together at the local hospital where she was a nurse and I was a radiologic technologist, and we had a lot of common interests. She was always encouraging me as a new mom and young wife. I always felt she was a true friend and wonderful Christian example of giving her best to others and not judging them for where they might be struggling in life. We lost Joel's dad suddenly when he died at age 59 of a heart attack, but because we lived so close to his parents, Joel was able to step in and help his mom on the farm. Ironically, Joel had just learned to plant the crops before his dad died. Joel's dad had always taken care of planting the crops in past years, but in the spring before he died, he told Joel it was time for him to learn to plant the crops, so Joel did. It was almost as if he knew he wasn't going to be there to plant the crops that next spring. Like many fathers do when given the opportunity, he took the opportunity to teach a life lesson.

Then that fall, the day before Joel's dad died, he drove on our yard to show us his "nearly new" John Deere 4440 tractor he had just purchased. He loved to show up at our place unannounced, but it made me smile. So I quickly grabbed our video camera to capture the moments as Grandpa held our daughter on his lap and gave her a ride on his new tractor. He was gone 24 hours later. We never know what God has in store, but what a beautiful legacy of love he left for his family.

One thing I admired about Joel's mom is that it seemed she was always filled with so much grace. During the years she was widowed, she didn't become bitter at her circumstances; rather, she continued to be there for us, and Joel was able to help her on the farm, too. For several months after Joel's dad passed away, she wrote in a journal that I had given her for Christmas. I find it comforting to read the daily entries she wrote about her journey after losing her best friend and husband, "H-ward," as she would lovingly call him. I knew that God placed us so close to Joel's parents for a purpose—to take care of one another—and sometimes we just have to trust in God's perfect plan for our lives, even when it doesn't always make sense to us.

Sometimes we just have to trust in God's perfect plan for our lives, even when it doesn't always make sense to us.

Five years after we lost Joel's dad, his mom died of a brain tumor on her husband's birthday. She fought a valiant fight, and I am so grateful to her for being such a great example of grace and unconditional love to my children and me. She was a sweet, yet strong Sherpa in my life who mentored me through motherhood and my faith!

MY SPIRITUAL SHERPAS

My husband's Grandpa Wally was a beacon to so many addicts and alcoholics in the dozens of years he worked at a rehab center.

He had been sober since the day after Joel was born. He found his true calling in helping others out of the prison of addiction, but he was also there for us early in our marriage to encourage us in our struggles.

Another great mentoring relationship in my life was with Pastor Don and Myra. Joel and I met this couple when we were invited by Joel's boss and friend, Dan, to a small church in the little town of Lester. We found a great community with young families like ours who were all involved in Sunday school and Bible studies. Pastor Don and his wife, Myra, modeled a wonderful and committed Christian marriage, and I'm grateful to them for mentoring and praying for our children and family for many years. They taught us the importance of the power of prayer and staying involved in a church family.

MY PROFESSIONAL SHERPAS

In my business and career life, I was fortunate to work with some incredible mentors. I will always be grateful for my friend Mark, who served as a great mentor to me and believed in my ability to become a leader long before I did. It was so important to my development as a leader! He saw potential in me that I didn't even know was there.

In large trainings, I used to be the girl in the back of the conference room, thinking to myself, "Wow! I hope I can be successful at this business someday, but please, God, don't you ever put me up on that stage!" But my friend Mark had other plans. At a smaller local training, he encouraged me to get up in front of the room and do part of the presentation. It was scary, and my knees were shaking, but taking that leap showed me I could do it, and I did! Mark continued to remind me, "You can do this!" He nudged me out of my nest, and I'm grateful for that.

He helped me spread my wings and learn to fly, setting me on a career path of speaking in front of others on a much bigger stage. I began to feel it was my calling to inspire others to be brave and overcome their doubts and fears, just as I was overcoming my fear of public speaking.

My co-worker and dear friend, Sharon, was also a strong mentor in my professional career. She was like my "work mom" who always supported me when I was ready to quit and give up on my dreams. She was a great encourager who knew I was fearful to step out of my comfort zone but empowered me to do so anyway. I was afraid to travel to conferences without my husband, but she would remind me that I wasn't alone and helped me to find the courage and, like they say, feel the fear and do it anyway!

There were many others along my career who were mentors in overcoming my fears and stepping out of my comfort zone with faith. With these people by my side, I began a journey from a stagnant career to becoming the purpose-filled, empowered woman that I had always longed to be! My Sherpas, my mentors helped me to become the person I wanted to become.

Who has guided you along the way? Who believes in you and has helped you grow? When you were in your own dark and vulnerable places in life, who helped you find your way? Recognize who these people are, honor them, and welcome them into your life, for they are your Sherpas.

CHAPTER 5: REFLECTIONS

1. List your Sherpas, and offer them thanks.

2. Have you served as a Sherpa in someone's life? How so?

3. What is important to you in a mentor?

6

INTEGRITY, A REFLECTION
OF WHO YOU ARE

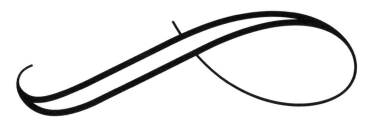

For years, Joel and I had completely separate careers. While I supported his work on the farm and he supported my work, we weren't working together. We gave one another the freedom each of us needed to do our own thing, and it worked for us.

Today, we are having so much more fun, as we not only found a way to work together but became a team. It has changed our relationship! We are fortunate to travel and build relationships within our business together, and Joel feels valued, too, because he's the spouse and the farmer who can offer a different perspective. People value his input and seeing that makes me proud.

> Today, we are having so much more fun, as we not only found a way to work together but became a team.

Most importantly, we are modeling a positive work relationship to our children. We have always had the common vision to raise our kids with good Christian values, but now they get to watch us build dreams together, too.

Before talking about the importance of discovering your full leadership potential, I want to talk about how powerful it can be to build a business with your spouse. How rewarding to work with someone you love, respect, and trust! Working with Joel has made my career richer and fuller, and it's been so fulfilling to have a common goal together. Sharing the workload and the income has shifted our perspective. We are humbled and grateful to be a team both in and out of the home, and we empower one another to be our best selves.

Whether working with your spouse or anyone you love and respect, consider collaboration in any way you can. There is power when you fully commit to working as a team!

MY LEADERSHIP PHILOSOPHY

I am so grateful that God has blessed me with an amazing family and an amazing team in my professional life. Fear used to be my stronghold! But, thankfully, I have faced my fears and choose courage over fear today. And guess what? We are all flawed! We all have doubts and shortcomings and stuff to overcome, but when you hold up that imaginary mirror, what do you see in your reflection? It is the mix of the good and bad habits or behaviors we possess. You see the good, the bad, and the ugly. What you see in the mirror is someone who can grow and lead. You are enough.

Good leaders are not born, they are made. By walking your talk, you become the person whom others want to follow. Leadership has great responsibility because "to whom much has been given, much will be required." (Luke 12:48)

It is time to step into your greatness and find the leader in you. What does your R.E.F.L.E.C.T.I.O.N. say about you?

R Stands for Responsibility

Take ownership and responsibility for your actions and inactions in your business and how it's progressing. No blaming or excuses: the buck stops with you! Know what you can change and what is out of your control.

In times of responsibility, I always look to the Serenity Prayer: "*God, grant me the serenity to accept the things I cannot change, the courage to change the things I can, and the wisdom to know the difference.*" Remember, there are some things we can't control in life and business, so it's best to focus on the things we CAN control.

HOW ARE YOU RESPONSIBLE, AND HOW CAN YOU BETTER PRACTICE RESPONSIBILITY?

E Stands for Empowerment

Empower yourself and others by having the GRACE to work on your failures and your shortcomings, and build on your strengths. Be a student of great leaders of personal development like Andy Andrews, John C. Maxwell, Jim Rohn, Darren Hardy, or Bob Proctor.

And, most importantly, feed your mind and soul daily by reading books, and attending Bible studies and personal development seminars. These are keys to developing the leader inside you. In just a few minutes of reading or listening to uplifting messages each day, you can begin to build a champion mindset.

HOW ARE YOU EMPOWERED, AND HOW CAN YOU BETTER PRACTICE EMPOWERMENT?

F Stands for Fun

In your business, create a CULTURE of fun and enjoyment with your team! Develop contests or team-building activities to give everyone a sense of unity. Many people long to be part of something bigger than themselves, so create around you a sense of community for them. Remember the "what's in it for me" mindset? There are people who crave the feeling of community and belonging, and that is a powerful way to build a solid team and business.

HOW ARE YOU CREATING A CULTURE OF FUN, AND HOW CAN YOU BETTER PRACTICE ENJOYMENT?

L Stands for Love

Season your business with LOVE. When you struggle to see through a situation that seems difficult or unfair, look at it with an attitude of love. When we come from a place of love, it changes us personally as well as our business, and the love approach is much less confrontational. Love never fails. I always say, walk a few miles in their shoes, and you will see a new perspective of where they are coming from.

HOW ARE YOU LOVING, AND HOW CAN YOU BETTER PRACTICE AN ATTITUDE OF LOVE?

E Stands for Energy

Manage your ENERGY and your VIBE! Positive or negative, others can sense your energy as soon as you enter a room, so you must have good energy to be successful. Your vibe attracts your tribe!

SMILE! Your personality and energy are reflected in your appearance, which means it's also important to dress for success. I was told early in my career to dress one level up from what your audience will be, and I find that so helpful. Studies actually show that when you are "dressed up" you actually perform better at your job or in your career.

HOW ARE YOU PRACTICING A POSITIVE VIBE, AND HOW CAN YOU IMPROVE?

C Stands for Commitment

Leaders are steadfast in doing what they say they are going to do to the best of their ability. They are committed to their goals because they have to be if they want to be successful. Always do what you say you're going to do. Be a person that follows through to the best of your ability. People will appreciate your commitment and will follow your lead.

HOW ARE YOU COMMITTED, AND HOW CAN YOU BETTER PRACTICE COMMITMENT?

T Stands for Time Management

This is not easy in today's world of distractions, but time management is crucial. Time is money! To achieve control of your hours in a day, track your income-producing activities and daily method of operation by prioritizing your day. Hold yourself accountable to a minimum of 30 minutes of an income-producing activity each day, and find an accountability partner to hold you to this.

HOW ARE YOU MANAGING YOUR TIME, AND HOW CAN YOU IMPROVE?

I Stands for Integrity

Be authentic to who you are! "To thine own self be true" is a favorite quote that reminds me to stay true to my authentic self. When you are a genuine and honest person, you build trust with your team. Never compromise your core beliefs, and people will respect you for that. Servant leaders reflect professionalism at all times and are always a "GO GIVER."

HOW ARE YOU AUTHENTIC, AND HOW CAN YOU IMPROVE?

O Stands for Overcome

Just like I did, it's time to overcome your fears! Fears are a prison that hold you captive from your fullest potential. I have faced my fears and forced myself to say YES when, deep down, I would have rather said No! But I said YES, and you can, too. Step out in faith to choose courage over fear.

Stepping out of your comfort zone provides the greatest blessing in the long run, so stop hiding behind your doubts and self-limiting beliefs, and be brave! "Find a way instead of an excuse" and see where this mantra will take you. I like Mel Robbins' "5 Second Rule" principle. If you count down 5-4-3-2-1 and do what you are afraid to DO, it can be a launching pad to help you overcome obstacles in your life and career. Action is a powerful tool in breaking the fear cycle.

HOW ARE YOU OVERCOMING YOUR FEARS, AND WHAT DO YOU NEED TO WORK ON?

N Stands for No Regrets

No matter how long this journey may take you, there is growth at work, and you *are* making progress. When you practice self-development and follow your heart, you are building your best self. Take time to enjoy the journey! Looking back on your life, how many times do you remember the moments and experiences along the way to your destination were the best part?

ARE YOU REGRET FREE? HOW CAN YOU GET THERE?

Our Pastor once spoke about staying "on course" in our spiritual and personal life. He shared how a compass uses "magnetic declination" to find a true north in seeking direction. I find that so important to us on our journey and in all aspects of our lives. I've always tried to remember my own "True North" on my life's journey as well. It's so easy to get distracted, but I remind myself WHY I said YES to my marriage, to my business decisions, and to my spiritual commitments.

Why did you say yes in the first place? What's your "True North" that keeps you engaged in your purpose each day? Stay in your "True North," and live with no regrets!

CHAPTER 6: REFLECTIONS

1. How do you commit to your family? How do you work together?

2. **How have you grown as a leader?**

3. What steps in self-development can you begin taking today?
   List them here.

7

THE EMPOWERED WOMAN

Because you picked up this book, I am confident there is an Empowered Woman within you, and I want to help you find her. But, ironically, The Empowered Woman begins when you're in a place feeling UNempowered. When I was in a lonely place, I felt vulnerable, confused, unsure, and insecure, so I can relate to you wherever you are in your own darkness. But I was set free from that bondage, and you can be, too.

Who is The Empowered Woman? She is someone who takes time to discover who she really is. As busy moms or as busy businesswomen, we often take care of everybody else around us, but The Empowered Woman knows that if you want to give your best self, you have to take care of yourself, too. When you take time to be healthy and strong, you are going to better

> **The Empowered Woman begins when you're in a place feeling UNempowered.**

serve others. Some people might think it's selfish to take some time for yourself, but I disagree. Our bodies are a temple, and we should take care of it! That's what God wants us to do. We cannot give what we don't have. If we are not well, we cannot be a gift to someone else, and The Empowered Woman understands and respects this. She makes time to take care of herself so that she can better care for others.

The Empowered Woman does not let people take advantage of her. Instead, she is strong enough and respects herself enough to say NO when she needs to and reminds others of her healthy boundaries. She is willing to help others but understands that setting boundaries is wise and important.

Do you remember who you were as a five-year-old dreamer? Who you were out at recess time when you simply did what you loved with reckless abandon? The Empowered Woman knows how to get back to that girl somehow, because that is who she truly is—where the grass is greener, the sky is bluer, and everything in life makes sense. Where your "talents and your passion" intersect and you feel your soul is "on fire" with purpose—that is your "Zone of Genius," and The Empowered Woman lives there.

The Empowered Woman serves others and lives an authentic life. She helps people feel important and valued. When she interacts with people, she takes time to find common

The Empowered Woman honors this and knows that seeing a gift in someone can really help them feel good about themselves, and that gift matters!

ground and build rapport. I remember reading about Mary Kay Ash's philosophy, pretending that everyone you meet has a sign around their neck that reads, "Make Me Feel Important." The Empowered Woman honors this and knows that seeing a gift in someone can really help them feel good about themselves, and that gift matters! She loves learning and seeking to improve on her weaknesses and building her strengths. As it says in Proverbs 31: "She is clothed in strength and dignity, laughs without fear of the future, when she speaks her words are wise, and she gives instructions with kindness."

THE BUSINESS MODEL FOR THE EMPOWERED WOMAN

Committed to her goals—She perseveres and is patient with the process.

Mentored—She doesn't try to do it all alone. She asks for help.

Disciplined—She has great work ethic and is driven to be her best self.

A "Lady Boss"—She uses her skill set and energy to create multiple or residual streams of income in a flexible work-from-anywhere environment! She can give herself a "salary increase" while working a part-time business on the side.

Equipped—Lastly, she is **always learning** and growing spiritually, personally, and professionally.

Begin nurturing The Empowered Woman within you today! You are enough. You have what it takes.

ARE YOU QUALIFIED?

This question defines our choices in life, doesn't it? Are you qualified as a Christian? Are you qualified as a wife or a mother? Are you qualified in your career? It seems we are always striving to be QUALIFIED in our roles in life. When I discovered residual income and network marketing, it was so refreshing to see that people from all walks of life were qualified in this industry to go as far as they wanted to in terms of financial success. There was no specific person or set of characteristics to be successful.

Instead, I learned that I could become successful starting right where I was. And what was inspiring to me was the thought of helping others do the same. Anyone could set goals and succeed regardless of their formal education or background. Not just one type of person but, by on-the-job training, everyone was qualified to earn while we learn!

Today, the Internet is really replacing how we shop, and the marketplace is expanding globally through network marketing and e-commerce. Did you know that in the next 5 years, 80% of women who earn over $100,000 a year will do so in a direct sales/social marketing or home-based business? That's so encouraging!

The "side hustle" has become the wave of the future, and it makes sense now to have multiple streams of income for financial security. Many of us also become stagnant in our careers after 20 or 30 years and are looking for a change of pace. With a good social marketing or direct sales company that has the right timing and product line, you can reach new horizons in your career as you discover your new purpose in life!

If your goal is to work from home, meet new people, expand your horizons, or create a second stream of income to help with expenses or retirement or get out of debt, I strongly encourage you to seek out a good network marketing company. If you're not inclined to sales or network marketing, then start a service or develop a product that fills a need. Do you enjoy networking, baking cupcakes, cooking meals, coaching, or making crafts? What specific skills do you have that others don't? I love the fact that Uber is the largest taxi service yet they don't own any vehicles. Think outside the box on where you can provide a service or skill to others, develop a plan of action, and then execute it!

> **I strongly encourage you to seek out a good network marketing company.**

We have a lake cabin that we like to visit on the weekends, and I love seeing the ice cream truck ring his bell and drive through the neighborhood. What a smart guy! He thought, *Hey, it's hot out, and a cold ice cream treat would really hit the spot right now; why not bring the ice cream treat directly to the consumer?* He saw a need, and he filled it! Think of what you really thrive on—where your skills collide with the one thing that really "blows your hair back"—then create it, build it, and DO IT!

BEGIN PERSONAL DEVELOPMENT

Years ago, I was afraid, insecure, and worried what others thought of me. Today, I'm a different person—an Empowered Woman—because I conceded to God's unconditional love. I chose courage over fear, and I began the path of personal development to build my belief in myself and the power of God's Plan for my life. With discipline and discernment for my purpose to empower others to discover their God-given talents and gifts. Today, I want to help you on your journey to greatness!

Personal development takes action. Take just one small step each day, be proactive, take time to reflect, build your skill set, and surround yourself with Sherpas who believe in you. Get rid of negative thoughts and negative people in your life and, instead, feed your mind with positive things. Stop filling your days with "busyness," and start feeding your soul with encouragement!

MY TOP 3 PERSONAL DEVELOPMENT HABITS

1. **Set Your Mindset Each Day**—Offer gratitude through a journal or prayerful affirmations. "Be still and Know that I am GOD." (Psalm 46:10)
2. **Have Accountability**—Find an accountability partner, and keep in touch. Encourage each other! We don't do life alone.
3. **Daily Method of Operation**—Set and accomplish at least one goal each day. Do one positive thing! Small steps build success. As the old saying goes, "Life by the inch is a cinch, life by the yard is hard." So take one step at a time!

Some people can be so overwhelmed in their lives that they don't even want to get out of bed in the morning, but just one small victory can be a step toward changing everything. I took small steps toward victory when I started traveling by myself and presented in front of our small meeting group. I took the step in faith and faced my giants! Those small steps led to great victories. You can do the same. What small step can you take, despite your fear?

When we allow fear to paralyze us, it's because we're making the thing we fear about *ourselves*. But when our purpose is doing what we fear *for others*, the burden is lifted! What can you give to somebody else? Make it about blessing them.

Most importantly, in your personal development, make room for God. I am a child of the King, a friend and a follower of Christ. I am thirsty for the authentic life of the Empowered Christian Woman, and I aspire to equip you and help you break free from your own fear of doubt and insignificance. I want to help you discover your calling and your divine purpose for being here. I

> **Stop performing, and start abiding in His love and grace!**

want you to know that YOU MATTER, and you have special gifts and talents that are required to build God's Kingdom here on earth. Stop performing, and start abiding in His love and grace!

This is not a dress rehearsal; this is your life! When you finally begin the path of discovering your true self, there is an incredible peace and joy in that journey!

CHAPTER 7: REFLECTIONS

1. Where in your life were you feeling UNempowered? How did
    you prevail?

2.   What will it take for you to become an Empowered Woman?

3. **What are your personal development habits? List them here.**

FINAL THOUGHTS

As I finish this gift to you, I am approaching the "second act" of my life. I'm looking forward to becoming a grandmother for the first time and hopeful that I can be a loving and grace-filled grandparent to my grandchildren. But this time is also an opportunity to reflect on achievements and consider how to progress into being the best version of myself and living a congruent life of purpose and passion. It's an exciting time!

Sometimes life gives us "do overs," proving that we are always works in progress. We can't live our best life if we are constantly looking back! I love the verse from Lamentations: "*The steadfast love of the Lord never ceases; His mercies never come to an end, they are new every morning. Great is your faithfulness.*"

Perhaps you, too, are in the "second act" of your life or facing an "empty nest." It's going to be okay! I remember crying the entire four-hour trip home after dropping my son off at college. It's as if their entire lifetime flashes through your mind—you see the young man waving goodbye to you as you drive away from the dorm, but you swear he was just five years old taking that big step onto the yellow school bus for his first day of kindergarten! It happens in a flash.

After sending both my son and daughter off to college, I can assure you that you will adjust to your "empty nest" just fine. You did your job well! You raised them to become independent adults who are ready to set sail on their own course in life. Now it's time to find your new normal.

Reacquaint yourself with your spouse, and enjoy some well-deserved freedom. Breathe, exhale, and realize that you are ready for a new adventure! Pamper yourself with a spa day, meet some girlfriends for coffee or cocktails, schedule a weekend trip with your spouse or girlfriends. Think. What is it you really enjoy doing? Yes, you, that five-year-old-ready-for-recess YOU!

I have a little secret for you. If you are in your "second act" like me, you will soon realize that this stage of life is actually really fun and enjoyable! So start something new, join a new networking group, sign up to take a new class, or make a new friend. Do whatever it

> **Do whatever it takes to discover your purpose, find your courage and live out your calling.**

takes to discover your purpose, find your courage, and live out your calling. Remember, instead of filling your days with things that don't matter, start feeding your soul with things that do!

You can do all these things because YOU now have the Code to Grace. Do you know what it is? Of course, it is found in God's unconditional love. You now have the *courage* to *overcome* your fears as you *discover* that you have had the key to your life all along. Now go, and *empower* others to live a life on purpose!

To God Be the Glory …

ABOUT THE AUTHOR

Marilyn Moser is a maverick in the women's leadership arena! She's a wife and mother and lives her passion of empowering women. She enjoys mentoring and coaching her team and business colleagues, challenging them to become their best self. She has 30 years of experience in the health and wellness industry from radiology and mammography healthcare sciences to a former fitness instructor who believes in the proactive approach to wellness. She cherishes her family and loves traveling the world to live a life on purpose! She's a top leader in a global nutrigenomics company and enjoys training teams to maximize their earning potential as they grow their influence. Marilyn is excited to be writing her first book on women entrepreneurship and empowerment and to give her success tips on becoming an authentic entrepreneur.

ABOUT THE COMPANY

LifeVantage

I feel incredibly blessed and honored to achieve the rank of Pro 7 with the efforts of my amazing team! LifeVantage has offered me so many wonderful blessings and the opportunity to experience personal growth on a whole new level. The wonderful friendships that I've made during my LifeVantage journey have enriched my life in countless ways.

Five years ago, I was introduced to this amazing opportunity with no idea how much I truly needed this business. I was facing the "empty nest" and maxed out in my career as a full time radiologic technologist and mammography coordinator. Facing cutbacks in my salary at the medical center where I worked, LifeVantage provided a vehicle to change my financially-stagnant career and create an extra stream of income while working part-time. As a result, my husband was able to retire from his plumbing business and enjoy farming and ranching full-time. Last May, I also retired from my full-time job as a mammography coordinator!

It's time to create the life you were designed to live! With the help of LifeVantage, we are living with a new purpose and building a legacy for our family to enjoy for years to come. I'm forever grateful that LifeVantage was put in my path. Let's pay it forward and share this opportunity with everyone!